2/24

EASY
Vegetarian

EASY
Vegetarian

Love Food ® is an imprint of Parragon Books Ltd

Parragon
Queen Street House
4 Queen Street
Bath BA1 1HE, UK

Copyright © Parragon Books Ltd 2009

Love Food ® and the accompanying heart device is a trademark of Parragon Books Ltd

Additional photography by Clive Bozzard-Hill
Food styling by Val Barrett and Carol Tennent
Introduction by Anne Sheasby

ISBN: 978-1-4075-2869-4

Printed in Indonesia

NOTES FOR THE READER
This book uses imperial, metric, and US cup measurements. Follow the same units of measurement
throughout; do not mix imperial and metric. All spoon measurements are level, unless otherwise
stated: teaspoons are assumed to be 5 ml, and tablespoons are assumed to be 15 ml. Unless
otherwise stated, milk is assumed to be whole, eggs, and individual fruits such as bananas are
medium, and pepper is freshly ground black pepper.
Recipes using raw or very lightly cooked eggs should be avoided by children, the elderly, pregnant
women, convalescents, and anyone with a chronic condition.
Sufferers from nut allergies should be aware that some of the ready-prepared ingredients in the
recipes in this book may contain nuts. Pregnant and breast-feeding women are advised to avoid
eating peanuts and peanut products.
Readers should be aware that some of the ready-made ingredients, such as cheese, specified in the
recipes may contain animal products. Always check the packaging before use or purchase items from
specialist shops.

Contents

Introduction 6

1 Soups & Appetizers 8

2 Snacks & Light Meals 46

3 Main Dishes 84

4 Side Dishes 122

Index 160

Introduction

In many countries around the world, vegetarianism has been a way of life for centuries. People choose to be vegetarian for numerous different reasons, be it on religious or moral grounds, for health reasons, and so on.

Webster's Dictionary defines vegetarianism as "The practice of or belief in eating a diet made up chiefly of vegetables, grains, fruits, nuts, seeds, and occasionally, dairy products, as milk or cheese." A vegetarian is "a practitioner or advocate of vegetarianism."

Different Types of Vegetarian Diets

There are several different kinds of vegetarian diets. Lacto-ova-vegetarians, the most common type of vegetarians, avoid meat, poultry, fish, etc, but they do eat both dairy products and eggs. Lacto-vegetarians avoid meat, poultry, fish, etc, as well as eggs, but they do eat dairy products. Vegans do not eat meat, poultry, and fish, etc, nor dairy products, eggs, or any other animal product. Fruitarians and those following a macrobiotic diet also come under the umbrella of vegetarian diets and these eating plans are even more restrictive.

Vegetarian Diet & Health

A typical vegetarian diet is generally a healthy way of eating as it tends to be naturally low in saturated fat (as long as not too much cheese is eaten), and high in dietary fiber and starchy carbohydrate foods. A vegetarian diet includes a wide range of foods such as beans and legumes, cereals and grains, nuts and seeds, fruit, vegetables, dairy foods, soy products, and eggs (depending on the type of vegetarian diet). Following a balanced, healthy vegetarian eating plan, and including some foods from each group every day, should provide vegetarians with the correct balance of foods and all the nutrients, vitamins, and minerals that they need to keep healthy.

Vegetables and fruit play an important role in vegetarian cooking, adding not only vibrant colors and varied textures and flavors, but also vital vitamins and minerals (such as vitamins A, C, and E, iron, zinc, and other trace elements), dietary fiber, and cancer-protecting antioxidant nutrients.

A wide range of beans and legumes are readily available (either dried or canned), as well as cereals and grains such as pasta (both fresh and dried), rice, bulgur wheat, cornmeal, couscous, quinoa, etc, all of which form the basis of many tempting vegetarian dishes and provide complex carbohydrates, dietary fiber, vitamins, and minerals, and some provide a valuable source of protein too.

Nuts and seeds are an ideal way to increase the texture and taste of many recipes while adding important nutrients too. Dairy foods, eggs, and soy products provide essential protein needed for the growth and repair of all body cells.

Vegetarian Cooking

Successful vegetarian cooking can be achieved by combining the wide variety of foods and ingredients available, to create exciting and tempting dishes from all corners of the globe. Vegetarian cooking doesn't need to be complicated. Quite often the simpler the dish and the less preparation and cooking involved, the better, especially when using fresh produce such as vegetables.

The versatility of many vegetables, not forgetting the humble potato, which is one of the most versatile of all vegetables, means that they lend themselves to creativity in the kitchen. Fresh herbs and spices are also a great way of adding flavor and interest to dishes.

Try experimenting with different ingredients and foods that perhaps you haven't tried before. For example, combine protein-packed beans or legumes with a selection of fresh, colorful vegetables to create a rich, warming winter stew or a light and refreshing summer salad.

This cookbook will introduce you to a tempting selection of delicious and nutritious vegetarian recipes, many of which are quick and easy to make, and all of which will inspire you to create and enjoy vegetarian dishes.

The recipes are presented in four different chapters including Soups & Appetizers, Snacks & Light Meals, Main Dishes, and Side Dishes, offering an extensive choice of enticing recipes for all the family to enjoy.

1

Soups & Appetizers

Vegetable & Corn Chowder

serves 4

1 tbsp vegetable oil

1 red onion, diced

1 red bell pepper, seeded and diced

3 garlic cloves, crushed

1¾ cups diced potatoes

2 tbsp all-purpose flour

2½ cups milk

1¼ cups vegetable stock

½ cup broccoli florets

3 cups canned corn kernels, drained

¾ cup grated cheddar cheese, plus extra to garnish

salt and pepper

Heat the oil in a large pan. Add the onion, bell pepper, garlic, and potato and sauté over low heat, stirring frequently, for 2–3 minutes.

Stir in the flour and cook, stirring for 30 seconds. Gradually stir in the milk and stock.

Add the broccoli and corn kernels. Bring the mixture to a boil, stirring constantly, then reduce the heat and simmer for about 20 minutes, or until all the vegetables are tender.

Add ½ cup of the cheese and stir until it melts.

Season to taste and ladle into warmed bowls. Garnish with the remaining cheese and serve.

Creamy Tomato & Basil Soup

serves 6

2 tbsp butter

1 tbsp olive oil

1 onion, finely chopped

1 garlic clove, chopped

2 lb/900 g plum tomatoes, chopped

2¾ cups vegetable stock

½ cup dry white wine

2 tbsp sun-dried tomato paste

2 tbsp torn fresh basil leaves

⅔ cup heavy cream

salt and pepper

fresh basil leaves, to garnish

Melt the butter with the oil in a large, heavy-bottomed pan. Add the onion and cook, stirring occasionally, for 5 minutes, or until softened. Add the garlic, tomatoes, stock, wine, and tomato paste, stir well, and season to taste. Partially cover the pan and simmer, stirring occasionally, for 20–25 minutes, or until the mixture is soft and pulpy.

Remove the pan from the heat, leave to cool slightly, then pour into a blender or food processor. Add the torn basil and process. Push the mixture through a strainer into a clean pan with a wooden spoon.

Stir in the cream and reheat the soup, but do not let it boil. Ladle the soup into warmed bowls, garnish with the basil leaves and serve immediately.

Borscht

serves 6

1 onion

¼ cup butter

12 oz/350 g raw beets, cut into thin sticks, and 1 raw beet, grated

1 carrot, cut into thin sticks

3 celery stalks, thinly sliced

2 tomatoes, peeled, seeded and chopped

6¼ cups vegetable stock

1 tbsp white wine vinegar

1 tbsp sugar

2 large fresh dill sprigs

4 oz/115 g white cabbage, shredded

salt and pepper

⅔ cup sour cream, to garnish

Slice the onion into rings. Melt the butter in a large, heavy-bottomed pan. Add the onion and cook over low heat, stirring occasionally, for 3–5 minutes, or until softened. Add the sticks of beet, carrot, celery, and chopped tomatoes and cook, stirring frequently, for 4–5 minutes.

Add the stock, vinegar, and sugar and snip a tablespoon of dill into the pan. Season to taste with salt and pepper. Bring to a boil, reduce the heat and simmer for 35–40 minutes, or until the vegetables are tender.

Stir in the cabbage, cover, and simmer for 10 minutes, then stir in the grated beet, with any juices, and cook for an additional 10 minutes. Ladle the borscht into warmed bowls. Garnish with sour cream and another tablespoon of snipped dill and serve.

Carrot & Cumin Soup

serves 4–6

3 tbsp butter or margarine

1 large onion, chopped

1–2 garlic cloves, crushed

3 cups carrots, sliced

3¾ cups vegetable stock

¾ tsp ground cumin

2 celery stalks, thinly sliced

1 cup potato, diced

2 tsp tomato paste

2 tsp lemon juice

2 fresh or dried bay leaves

about 1¼ cups low-fat milk

salt and pepper

celery leaves, to garnish

Melt the butter or margarine in a large pan. Add the onion and garlic and cook very gently until softened.

Add the carrots and cook gently for a further 5 minutes, stirring frequently and taking care they do not brown.

Add the stock, cumin, seasoning, celery, potato, tomato paste, lemon juice, and bay leaves and bring to a boil. Cover and simmer for about 30 minutes until the vegetables are tender.

Remove and discard the bay leaves, cool the soup a little, and then press it through a strainer or process in a food processor or blender until smooth.

Pour the soup into a clean pan, add the milk, and bring to a boil over low heat. Taste and adjust the seasoning if necessary. Ladle into warmed bowls, garnish each serving with a small celery leaf and serve.

Bell Pepper & Chile Soup

serves 4

8 oz/225 g red bell peppers, seeded and sliced

1 onion, sliced

2 garlic cloves, crushed

1 green chile, chopped

1¼ cups strained tomatoes

2½ cups vegetable stock

2 tbsp chopped basil

shredded basil, to garnish

Put the red bell peppers in a large pan with the onion, garlic, and chile. Add the strained tomatoes and the vegetable stock and bring to a boil, stirring well.

Reduce the heat to a simmer and continue to cook the vegetables for 20 minutes, or until the bell peppers are soft. Drain, reserving the liquid and vegetables separately.

Using the back of a spoon, press the vegetables through a strainer. Alternatively, process in a food processor until smooth.

Return the vegetable purée to a clean pan with the reserved cooking liquid. Add the basil and heat through until hot. Garnish the soup with basil and serve immediately.

Mixed Bean Soup

serves 4

1 medium onion, chopped

1 garlic clove, finely chopped

2 celery stalks, sliced

1 large carrot, diced

14 oz/400 g canned chopped tomatoes

2/3 cup red wine

5 cups vegetable stock

1 tsp dried oregano

15 oz/425 g canned mixed beans and legumes

2 medium zucchini, diced

1 tbsp tomato paste

salt and pepper

store-bought pesto, to garnish

Place the prepared onion, garlic, celery, and carrot in a large pan. Stir in the tomatoes, red wine, vegetable stock, and oregano.

Bring the vegetable mixture to a boil, cover, and simmer for 15 minutes.

Stir the beans and zucchini into the mixture and continue to cook, uncovered, for a further 5 minutes.

Add the tomato paste to the mixture and season well with salt and pepper to taste.

Heat through, stirring occasionally, for a an additional 2–3 minutes, but do not let the mixture boil again.

Ladle the soup into warm bowls and serve, garnished with a spoonful of pesto.

Lettuce & Arugula Soup

serves 4–6

1 tbsp butter

1 large onion, halved and sliced

2 leeks, sliced

6¼ cups vegetable stock

6 tbsp white rice

2 carrots, thinly sliced

3 garlic cloves

1 bay leaf

2 heads soft round lettuce (about 1 lb/450 g), cored and chopped

¾ cup heavy cream

freshly grated nutmeg

3 oz arugula leaves, finely chopped

salt and pepper

Heat the butter in a large pan over medium heat and add the onion and leeks. Cover and cook for 3–4 minutes, stirring frequently, until the vegetables begin to soften.

Add the stock, rice, carrots, garlic, and bay leaf with a large pinch of salt. Bring just to a boil. Reduce the heat, cover, and simmer for 25–30 minutes, or until the rice and vegetables are tender. Remove the bay leaf.

Add the lettuce and cook for 10 minutes, until the leaves are softened, stirring occasionally.

Let the soup cool slightly, then transfer to a blender or food processor and purée until smooth, working in batches if necessary. (If using a food processor, strain off the cooking liquid and reserve. Purée the soup solids with enough cooking liquid to moisten them, then combine with the remaining liquid.)

Return the soup to the pan and place over medium-low heat. Stir in the cream and a grating of nutmeg. Simmer gently for about 5 minutes, stirring occasionally, until the soup is reheated. Add more water or cream if you prefer a thinner soup.

Add the arugula and simmer for 2–3 minutes, stirring occasionally, until it is wilted. Adjust the seasoning and ladle the soup into warm bowls.

Filo-Wrapped Asparagus

serves 4
for the dip

⅓ cup natural cottage cheese

1 tbsp low-fat milk

4 scallions, trimmed and finely chopped

2 tbsp chopped fresh mixed herbs, such as basil, mint, and tarragon

pepper

for the asparagus

20 asparagus spears

5 sheets filo dough

lemon wedges, to serve

Preheat the oven to 375°F/190°C. To make the dip, put the cottage cheese in a bowl and add the milk. Beat until smooth then stir in the scallions, chopped herbs, and pepper to taste. Place in a serving bowl, cover lightly, and chill in the refrigerator until required.

Cut off and discard the woody end of the asparagus and shave with a vegetable peeler to remove any woody parts from the spears.

Cut the filo dough into quarters and place one sheet on a clean counter. Brush lightly with water then place a spear at one end. Roll up to encase the spear, and place on a large baking sheet. Repeat until all the asparagus spears are wrapped in dough.

Bake for 10–12 minutes, or until the pastry is golden. Serve the spears with lemon wedges and the dip on the side.

Bell Pepper & Basil Stacks

serves 4

1 tsp olive oil

2 shallots, finely chopped

2 garlic cloves, crushed

pepper

2 red bell peppers, peeled, seeded, and sliced into strips

1 orange bell pepper, peeled, seeded, and sliced into strips

4 tomatoes, thinly sliced

2 tbsp shredded fresh basil

salad greens, to serve

Lightly brush 4 ramekin dishes with the oil. Mix the shallots and garlic together in a bowl and season with pepper to taste.

Layer the red and orange bell peppers with the tomatoes in the prepared ramekin dishes, sprinkling each layer with the shallot mixture and shredded basil. When all the ingredients have been added, cover lightly with plastic wrap or parchment paper. Weigh down using small weights and leave in the refrigerator for at least 6 hours, or preferably overnight.

When ready to serve, remove the weights and carefully run a knife around the edges. Invert onto serving plates and serve with salad greens.

Mushroom Pâté

serves 4

scant ¼ cup dried porcini
mushrooms

1 tsp olive oil

2 shallots, finely chopped

2 garlic cloves, crushed

1 fresh jalapeño chile,
seeded and finely
chopped

2 celery stalks, trimmed
and finely chopped

8 oz/225 g button
mushrooms, wiped and
sliced

grated rind and juice of
1 orange

½ cup fresh breadcrumbs

1 tbsp chopped fresh
parsley

1 small egg, beaten

pepper

raw vegetables sticks and
crisp breads, to serve

Preheat the oven to 350°F/180°C. Put the dried mushrooms in a bowl and cover with freshly boiled water. Let soak for 30 minutes then drain, chop, and set aside.

Heat the oil in a medium heavy-bottom pan, then add the shallots, garlic, chile, and celery. Cook, stirring frequently for 3 minutes, then add both the dried and fresh mushrooms and cook for an additional 2 minutes.

Add the orange juice and continue to cook for 3–4 minutes, or until the mushrooms have collapsed. Remove the pan from the heat and stir in the orange rind, breadcrumbs, parsley, beaten egg, and pepper to taste. Mix well.

Spoon the mixture into 4 individual ramekin dishes and level the surfaces. Place the dishes in a small baking pan and pour enough water to come halfway up the sides of the ramekins.

Cook for 15–20 minutes, or until a skewer inserted in the center of each ramekin comes out clean. Remove and either let stand for 10 minutes before serving warm or chill until ready to serve. Turn out and serve with vegetable sticks and crisp breads.

Stuffed Eggplant Slices

serves 4

1 medium eggplant

4 tbsp extra virgin olive oil

1 cup grated mozzarella cheese

1 tbsp fresh chopped basil

14 oz/400 g canned, chopped tomatoes with added herbs

extra basil leaves, to garnish

Preheat the oven to 400°F/200°C.

Slice the eggplant lengthwise into 8 slices. Brush the slices with oil and place on a baking sheet. Bake for 10 minutes, without letting them get too floppy. Remove from the oven. Sprinkle the grated cheese and basil over the eggplant slices.

Roll up each slice and place the slices in a single layer in a shallow ovenproof dish. Pour the chopped tomatoes over them and cook in the oven for 10 minutes or until the sauce bubbles and the cheese melts.

Remove the stuffed eggplant slices from the oven and transfer carefully to serving plates. Spoon any remaining chopped tomatoes on or around the eggplant slices. Garnish with basil leaves and serve while still hot.

Quesadillas

serves 4

4 tbsp finely chopped fresh
jalapeño chiles

1 onion, chopped

1 tbsp red wine vinegar

5 tbsp extra virgin olive oil

10½–14 oz/300–400 g
canned corn

8 soft flour tortillas

Put the chiles, onion, vinegar, and 4 tablespoons of olive oil in a food processor and process until finely chopped.

Tip into a bowl and stir in the corn.

Heat the remaining oil in a skillet, add a tortilla, and cook for 1 minute until golden.

Spread a quarter of the chile mixture over the tortilla and fold over.

Cook for 2–3 minutes until golden and the filling is heated through. Remove from the skillet and keep warm. Repeat with the other tortillas and filling. Serve immediately.

Creamed Mushrooms

serves 4

juice of 1 small lemon

1 lb/450 g small button mushrooms

2 tbsp butter

1 tbsp sunflower or olive oil

1 small onion, finely chopped

½ cup whipping or heavy cream

1 tbsp chopped fresh parsley, plus 4 sprigs to garnish

salt and pepper

Sprinkle a little of the lemon juice over the mushrooms.

Heat the butter and oil in a skillet, add the onion, and cook for 1 minute. Add the mushrooms, shaking the skillet so they do not stick.

Season with salt and pepper to taste, then stir in the cream, chopped parsley, and remaining lemon juice.

Heat until hot but don't let boil, then transfer to a serving plate and garnish with the parsley sprigs. Serve immediately.

Vegetable Tartlets

makes 12 tartlets

butter, for greasing

12 ready-baked pastry shells

2 tbsp olive oil

1 red bell pepper, seeded and diced

1 garlic clove, crushed

1 small onion, finely chopped

8 oz/225 g ripe tomatoes, chopped

1 tbsp torn fresh basil

1 tsp fresh or dried thyme

salt and pepper

green salad, to serve

Preheat the oven to 400°F/200°C and grease several baking sheets.

Place the ready-baked pastry shells on the prepared baking sheets.

Heat the oil in a skillet, add the bell pepper, garlic, and onion, and cook over high heat for about 3 minutes until soft.

Add the tomatoes, herbs, and seasoning and spoon onto the pastry shells.

Bake for about 5 minutes, or until the filling is piping hot. Serve warm with a green salad.

Eggplant Pâté

serves 4–6

2 large eggplants

4 tbsp extra virgin olive oil

2 garlic cloves, very finely chopped

4 tbsp lemon juice

salt and pepper

6 crisp breads, to serve

Preheat the oven to 350°F/180°C. Score the skins of the eggplants with the point of a sharp knife, without piercing the flesh, and place them on a baking sheet. Bake for 1¼ hours, or until soft.

Remove the eggplants from the oven and leave until cool enough to handle. Cut them in half and, using a spoon, scoop out the flesh into a bowl. Mash the flesh thoroughly.

Gradually beat in the olive oil then stir in the garlic and lemon juice. Season with salt and pepper to taste. Cover with plastic wrap and store in the refrigerator until required. Serve with the crisp breads.

Tomato Bruschetta

serves 4

8 slices of rustic bread

4 garlic cloves, halved

8 plum tomatoes, peeled and diced

extra virgin olive oil, for drizzling

salt and pepper

fresh basil leaves, to garnish

Preheat the broiler. Lightly toast the bread on both sides. Rub each piece of toast with half a garlic clove and then return to the broiler for a few seconds.

Divide the diced tomatoes among the toasts. Season with salt and pepper to taste and drizzle with olive oil. Serve immediately, garnished with basil leaves.

Spring Rolls

makes 12

2 scallions, trimmed, plus a few more to garnish

5 dried Chinese mushrooms or fresh open-cap mushrooms

1 large carrot

2 oz/55 g canned bamboo shoots

2 oz/55 g Napa cabbage

2 tbsp vegetable oil, plus extra for deep-frying

generous 2 cups bean sprouts

1 tbsp soy sauce

12 spring roll wrappers

1 egg, beaten

salt

Place the mushrooms in a small bowl and cover with warm water. Let soak for 20–25 minutes, then drain and squeeze out the excess water. Remove the coarse centers and slice the mushroom caps thinly. Cut the carrot and bamboo shoots into very thin julienne strips. Chop the 2 scallions and shred the Napa cabbage.

Heat 2 tablespoons of oil in a preheated wok. Add the mushrooms, carrot, and bamboo shoots and stir-fry for 2 minutes. Add the scallions, Napa cabbage, bean sprouts, and soy sauce. Season to taste with salt and stir-fry for 2 minutes. Cool.

Divide the mixture into 12 equal portions and place one portion on the edge of each spring roll wrapper. Fold in the sides and roll each one up, brushing the join with beaten egg to seal. Heat the oil for deep-frying in a large, heavy-bottomed pan to 350–375°F/180–190°C, or until a cube of bread browns in 30 seconds. Add the spring rolls, in batches, and cook for 4–5 minutes, or until golden and crispy. Take care that the oil is not too hot or the rolls will brown on the outside before cooking on the inside. Drain on paper towels. Keep warm. Garnish with the scallions and serve.

Hot Garlic-Stuffed Mushrooms

serves 4

4 large portobello mushrooms

4 sprays olive oil

2–3 garlic cloves, crushed

2 shallots

½ cup fresh whole wheat breadcrumbs

few fresh basil sprigs, plus extra to garnish

scant ¼ cup plumped dried apricots, chopped

1 tbsp pine nuts

2 oz/55 g feta cheese

pepper

Preheat the oven to 350°F/180°C. Remove the stalks from the mushrooms and set aside. Spray the bases of the mushrooms with the oil and place undersides up in a roasting pan.

Put the mushroom stalks in a food processor with the garlic, shallots, and breadcrumbs. Set aside a few basil sprigs for the garnish then place the remainder in the food processor with the apricots, pine nuts, and feta cheese. Add pepper to taste.

Process for 1–2 minutes, or until a stuffing consistency is formed, then divide among the mushroom caps.

Bake for 10–12 minutes, or until the mushrooms are tender and the stuffing is crisp on the top. Serve garnished with the reserved basil sprigs.

Snacks &
Light Meals

Red Onion, Tomato & Herb Salad

serves 4

2 lb/900 g tomatoes, sliced thinly

1 tbsp sugar (optional)

1 red onion, sliced thinly

large handful coarsely chopped fresh herbs

salt and pepper

for the dressing

2–4 tbsp vegetable oil

2 tbsp red wine vinegar or fruit vinegar

Arrange the tomato slices in a shallow bowl. Sprinkle with sugar (if using), salt, and pepper.

Separate the onion slices into rings and sprinkle them over the tomatoes. Sprinkle the herbs over the top. Any fresh herbs that are in season can be used—for example, tarragon, sorrel, cilantro, or basil.

Place the dressing ingredients in a jar with a screw-top lid. Shake well. Pour the dressing over the salad and mix gently.

Cover with plastic wrap and chill for 20 minutes. Remove the salad from the refrigerator 5 minutes before serving, unwrap the dish, and stir gently before setting out on the table.

Potato, Leek & Feta Patties

serves 4

1 whole garlic bulb

4 oz/115 g sweet potatoes, peeled and cut into chunks

6 oz/175 g carrots, peeled and chopped

4 oz/115 g leeks, trimmed and finely chopped

2 oz/55 g feta cheese, crumbled

1–2 tsp Tabasco sauce, or to taste

1 tbsp chopped fresh cilantro

pepper

fresh herbs or salad, to garnish

tomato ketchup, to serve (optional)

Preheat the oven to 375°F/190°C.

Break the garlic bulb open, place in a small roasting pan, and roast for 20 minutes, or until soft. Remove and when cool enough to handle, squeeze out the roasted garlic flesh.

Cook the sweet potatoes and carrots in a large pan of boiling water for 15 minutes, or until soft. Drain and mash then mix in the roasted garlic flesh.

Add the leeks, feta cheese, Tabasco sauce, cilantro, and pepper, to taste, to the potato mixture. Cover and let chill in the refrigerator for at least 30 minutes.

Using slightly dampened hands, shape the sweet potato mixture into 8 small round patties and place on a nonstick baking sheet. Bake for 15–20 minutes, or until piping hot. Garnish with fresh herbs or salad and serve with tomato ketchup, if using.

Zucchini, Carrot & Tomato Frittata

serves 4

2 sprays olive oil

1 onion, cut into small wedges

1–2 garlic cloves, crushed

2 eggs

2 egg whites

1 zucchini, about 3 oz/85 g, trimmed and grated

2 carrots, about 4 oz/115 g, peeled and grated

2 tomatoes, chopped

pepper

1 tbsp shredded fresh basil, for sprinkling

Heat the oil in a large nonstick skillet, add the onion and garlic, and sauté for 5 minutes, stirring frequently. Beat the eggs and egg whites together in a bowl then pour into the skillet. Using a spatula or fork, pull the egg mixture from the sides of the skillet into the center, allowing the uncooked egg to take its place.

Once the base has set lightly, add the grated zucchini and carrots with the tomatoes. Add pepper to taste and continue to cook over low heat until the eggs are set to personal preference.

Sprinkle with the shredded basil, cut the frittata into quarters and serve.

Spicy Stuffed Bell Peppers

serves 4

4 assorted colored bell peppers

3 sprays olive oil

1 onion, finely chopped

2 garlic cloves, chopped

1-inch/2.5-cm piece fresh ginger, peeled and grated

1–2 fresh serrano chiles, seeded and chopped

1 tsp ground cumin

1 tsp ground coriander

scant ½ cup cooked brown basmati rice

1 large carrot, about 4 oz/115 g, peeled and grated

1 large zucchini, about 3 oz/85 g, trimmed and grated

scant ¼ cup plumped dried apricots, finely chopped

1 tbsp chopped fresh cilantro

⅔ cup water

pepper

fresh herbs, to garnish

Preheat the oven to 375°F/190°C. Cut the tops off the bell peppers and set aside. Discard the seeds from each pepper. Place the peppers in a large bowl and cover with boiling water. Let soak for 10 minutes then drain and set aside.

Heat a nonstick skillet and spray with the oil. Add the onion, garlic, ginger, and chiles and sauté for 3 minutes, stirring frequently. Sprinkle in the ground spices and continue to cook for an additional 2 minutes.

Remove the skillet from the heat and stir in the rice, carrot, zucchini, apricots, chopped cilantro, and pepper to taste. Stir well, then use to stuff the peppers.

Place the stuffed peppers in an ovenproof dish large enough to allow the peppers to stand upright. Put the reserved tops in position. Pour the water around their bases, cover loosely with the lid or foil, and cook for 25–30 minutes, or until piping hot. Serve garnished with herbs.

Tomato Ratatouille

serves 4

4 sprays olive oil

1 onion, cut into small wedges

2–4 garlic cloves, chopped

1 small eggplant, trimmed and chopped

1 small red bell pepper, seeded and chopped

1 small yellow bell pepper, seeded and chopped

1 zucchini, trimmed and chopped

2 tbsp tomato paste

3 tbsp water

4 oz/115 g mushrooms, sliced if large

8 oz/225 g ripe tomatoes, chopped

pepper

1 tbsp shredded fresh basil, to garnish

1 oz/25 g Parmesan cheese, freshly shaved, to serve

Heat the oil in a heavy-bottom pan, add the onion, garlic, and eggplant and cook, stirring frequently for 3 minutes.

Add the peppers and zucchini. Mix the tomato paste and water together in a small bowl and stir into the pan. Bring to a boil, cover with a lid, reduce the heat to a simmer, and cook for 10 minutes.

Add the mushrooms and chopped tomatoes with pepper to taste and continue to simmer for 12–15 minutes, stirring occasionally, until the vegetables are tender.

Divide the ratatouille among 4 warmed bowls, garnish each with shredded basil, and serve with freshly shaved Parmesan cheese to sprinkle over.

Open Potato Omelet

serves 4

2 oz/55 g old potatoes, peeled and grated

1 onion, grated

2 garlic cloves, crushed

1 carrot, about 4 oz/115 g, peeled and grated

4 sprays olive oil

1 yellow bell pepper, peeled and thinly sliced

1 zucchini, about 3 oz/ 85 g, trimmed and thinly sliced

3 oz/85 g cherry tomatoes, halved

2 eggs

3 egg whites

1 tbsp snipped fresh chives

pepper

fresh arugula, to garnish

Put the grated potatoes into a large bowl and cover with cold water. Leave for 15 minutes then drain, rinse thoroughly, and dry on absorbent paper towels or a clean dishtowel. Mix with the grated onion, garlic, and carrot.

Heat a heavy-bottom nonstick skillet and spray with the oil. Add the potato, onion, garlic, and carrot mixture and cook over low heat for 5 minutes, pressing the vegetables down firmly with a spatula. Add the peeled bell pepper and zucchini slices. Cover with a lid or crumpled piece of foil and cook very gently, stirring occasionally, for 5 minutes.

Add the halved cherry tomatoes and cook for an additional 2 minutes, or until the vegetables are tender.

Beat the whole eggs, egg whites, pepper to taste, and the chives together in a bowl. Pour over the vegetable mixture and cook for 4–5 minutes, stirring the egg from the sides of the skillet toward the center, until the vegetables are tender and the eggs are set. Serve immediately, garnished with arugula leaves.

Green Bean & Walnut Salad

serves 2

1 lb/450 g beans

1 small onion, finely chopped

1 garlic clove, chopped

4 tbsp freshly grated Parmesan cheese

2 tbsp chopped walnuts or almonds, to garnish

for the dressing

3 tbsp extra virgin olive oil

2 tbsp white wine vinegar

2 tsp chopped fresh tarragon

salt and pepper

Trim the beans, but leave them whole. Cook for 3–4 minutes in salted boiling water. Drain well, refresh under cold running water, and drain again. Put into a mixing bowl and add the onion, garlic, and cheese.

Place the dressing ingredients in a jar with a screw-top lid. Shake well. Pour the dressing over the salad and toss gently to coat. Cover with plastic wrap and chill for at least 30 minutes.

Remove the beans from the refrigerator 10 minutes before serving. Give them a quick stir and transfer to an attractive, shallow serving dish.

Toast the nuts in a dry skillet over medium heat for 2 minutes, or until they begin to brown. Sprinkle the toasted nuts over the beans to garnish before serving.

Cheese Baked Zucchini

serves 4

4 medium zucchini

2 tbsp extra virgin olive oil

4 oz/115 g mozzarella cheese, sliced thinly

2 large tomatoes, seeded and diced

2 tsp chopped fresh basil or oregano

Preheat the oven to 400°F/200°C.

Slice the zucchini lengthwise into 4 strips each. Brush with oil and place on a baking sheet.

Bake the zucchini in the oven for 10 minutes without letting them get too floppy.

Remove the zucchini from the oven. Arrange the slices of cheese on top and sprinkle with diced tomato and basil or oregano. Return to the oven for 5 minutes, or until the cheese melts.

Remove the zucchini from the oven and transfer carefully to serving plates.

Nutty Beet Salad

serves 4

3 tbsp red wine vinegar or fruit vinegar

3 cooked beets, grated

2 sharp eating apples

2 tbsp lemon juice

4 large handfuls mixed salad greens, to serve

4 tbsp pecans, to garnish

for the dressing

¼ cup plain yogurt

¼ cup mayonnaise

1 garlic clove, chopped

1 tbsp chopped fresh dill

salt and pepper

Sprinkle vinegar over the beets, cover with plastic wrap, and chill for at least 4 hours.

Core and slice the apples, place the slices in a dish, and sprinkle with the lemon juice.

Combine the dressing ingredients in a small bowl. Remove the beets from the refrigerator and dress. Add the apples to the beets and mix gently to coat with the salad dressing.

To serve, arrange a handful of salad greens on each plate and top with a large spoonful of the apple and beet mixture.

Toast the pecans in a heavy, dry skillet over medium heat for 2 minutes, or until they begin to brown. Sprinkle them over the beets and apple to garnish.

Tomato & Feta Salad

serves 4

2 lb 4 oz/1 kg ripe
tomatoes, thickly sliced

8 oz/225 g feta cheese

½ cup extra virgin olive oil

16 black olives, pitted

pepper

Arrange the tomato slices in concentric rings on a serving dish. Crumble the feta over the tomatoes and drizzle with the olive oil. Top with the olives.

Season to taste with pepper. Salt is probably not necessary because feta is already quite salty. Let stand for 30 minutes before serving.

Goat Cheese Tarts

makes about 12 tarts

butter, for greasing

14 oz/400 g package prepared and rolled puff pastry

1 tbsp all-purpose flour

1 egg, beaten

3 tbsp onion relish or tomato relish

three 4 oz/115 g goat cheese logs, sliced

extra virgin olive oil, for drizzling

pepper

Preheat the oven to 400°F/200°C and grease several baking sheets.

Cut out as many 3-inch/7.5-cm circles as possible from the pastry on a lightly floured counter.

Place the circles on the baking sheets and press gently, about 1 inch/2.5 cm from the edge of each, with a smaller 2-inch/5-cm dough cutter.

Brush the circles with beaten egg and prick with a fork. Top each circle with a little relish and a slice of goat cheese. Drizzle with oil and sprinkle over a little black pepper.

Bake for 8–10 minutes, or until the pastry is crisp and the cheese is bubbling. Serve warm.

Falafel Burgers

serves 4

two 14 oz/400 g can
chickpeas, drained and
rinsed

1 small onion, chopped

zest and juice of 1 lime

2 tsp ground coriander

2 tsp ground cumin

6 tbsp all-purpose flour

4 tbsp olive oil

4 fresh basil sprigs,
to garnish

tomato salsa, to serve

Put the chickpeas, onion, lime zest and juice, and the spices into a food processor and process to a coarse paste.

Tip the mixture out onto a clean counter or cutting board and shape into 4 patties.

Spread the flour out on a large flat plate and use to coat the patties.

Heat the oil in a large skillet, add the burgers, and cook for 2 minutes on each side until crisp. Garnish with basil and serve with tomato salsa.

Wilted Spinach, Yogurt & Walnut Salad

serves 2

1 lb/450 g fresh spinach leaves

1 onion, chopped

1 tbsp olive oil

1 cup plain yogurt

1 garlic clove, finely chopped

2 tbsp chopped toasted walnuts

2–3 tsp chopped fresh mint

salt and pepper

pita bread, to serve

Put the spinach and onion into a pan, cover, and cook gently for a few minutes until the spinach has wilted.

Add the oil and cook for an additional 5 minutes. Season with salt and pepper to taste.

Combine the yogurt and garlic in a bowl.

Put the spinach and onion into a serving bowl and pour over the yogurt mixture. Scatter over the walnuts and chopped mint and serve with pita bread.

Baked Chile Cheese Sandwiches

makes 4 sandwiches

3½ cups grated cheese, such as cheddar

8 tbsp butter, softened, plus extra to finish

4 fresh green chiles, seeded and chopped

½ tsp ground cumin

8 thick slices bread

Preheat the oven to 375°F/190°C. Mix the cheese and butter together in a bowl until creamy then add the chiles and cumin.

Spread this mixture over 4 slices of bread and top with the remaining slices.

Spread the outside of the sandwiches with extra butter and bake for 8–10 minutes until crisp. Serve.

Broiled Provolone with Herbed Couscous

serves 4

1 lb/450 g provolone cheese, cut into ¼-inch/5-mm slices

4 tbsp chili oil

for the herbed couscous

1¾ cups hot vegetable stock

heaping 1 cup couscous

2 tbsp chopped fresh mixed herbs

2 tsp lemon juice

1 tbsp olive oil

Preheat the broiler to high and line the broiler rack with foil.

Put the cheese slices in a bowl, pour over the chili oil, and toss well to coat the cheese.

Place the cheese on the broiler rack and cook under the broiler for 2–3 minutes on each side until golden.

Meanwhile, stir the hot stock into the couscous in a large bowl. Cover and let stand for 5 minutes.

Stir the herbs, lemon juice, and olive oil into the couscous and serve with the broiled provolone cheese.

Nachos with Chiles & Olives

serves 4

2 lb 4 oz/1 kg tortilla chips

6 tbsp chopped pickled jalapeño chiles

⅔ cup black olives, pitted and sliced

1 lb/450 g cheddar cheese, grated

dipping sauce

Preheat the oven to 350°F/180°C. Spread out the tortilla chips in a large ovenproof dish.

Sprinkle the chiles, olives, and grated cheese evenly over the tortilla chips and bake for 12–15 minutes, or until the cheese is melted and bubbling. Serve immediately with a dipping sauce of your choice.

Warm Goat Cheese Salad

serves 4

1 small Iceberg lettuce, torn
into pieces

handful of arugula leaves

few radicchio leaves, torn

6 slices French bread

4 oz/115 g goat cheese,
sliced

for the dressing

4 tbsp extra virgin olive oil

1 tbsp white wine vinegar

salt and pepper

Preheat the broiler. Divide all the leaves among 4 individual salad bowls.

Toast one side of the bread under the broiler until golden. Place a slice of cheese on top of each untoasted side and toast until the cheese is just melting.

Put all the dressing ingredients into a bowl and beat together until combined. Pour over the leaves, tossing to coat.

Cut each slice of bread in half and place 3 halves on top of each salad. Toss very gently to combine and serve warm.

Moroccan Tomato & Red Bell Pepper Salad

serves 4

3 red bell peppers

4 ripe tomatoes

½ bunch of fresh cilantro, chopped

2 garlic cloves, finely chopped

salt and pepper

Preheat the broiler. Place the bell peppers on a baking sheet and cook under the broiler, turning occasionally, for 15 minutes. Add the tomatoes and broil, turning occasionally, for an additional 5–10 minutes, or until all the skins are charred and blistered. Remove from the heat and let cool.

Peel and seed the bell peppers and tomatoes and slice the flesh thinly. Place in a bowl, mix well, and season with salt and pepper. Sprinkle with the cilantro and garlic, cover with plastic wrap, and chill in the refrigerator for at least 1 hour. Just before serving, drain off any excess liquid.

Main
Dishes

Chile Broccoli Pasta

serves 4

2 cups dry penne or macaroni

1 medium head broccoli

¼ cup extra virgin olive oil

2 large garlic cloves, chopped

2 fresh red chiles, seeded and diced

8 cherry tomatoes (optional)

small handful of fresh basil or parsley, to garnish

salt

Cook the penne or other pasta in a large pan of salted boiling water for about 10 minutes, until tender but still firm to the bite. Remove from the heat, drain, rinse with cold water, and drain again. Set aside.

Cut the broccoli into florets and cook in salted boiling water for 5 minutes. Drain, rinse with cold water, and drain again.

Heat the olive oil in the pan that the pasta was cooked in. Add the garlic, chiles, and tomatoes, if using. Cook over high heat for 1 minute.

Return the broccoli to the pan with the oil and mix well. Cook for 2 minutes to heat through. Add the pasta and mix well again. Cook for 1 minute more.

Remove the pasta from the heat, turn into a large serving bowl, and serve garnished with basil or parsley.

Mushroom & Cauliflower Cheese Crumble

serves 4

1 medium cauliflower

¼ cup butter

1⅔ cups sliced white mushrooms

salt and pepper

for the topping

1⅔ cups dry breadcrumbs

2 tbsp grated Parmesan cheese

1 tsp dried oregano

1 tsp dried parsley

¼ cup butter

Bring a large pan of salted water to a boil.

Break the cauliflower into small florets and cook in the boiling water for 3 minutes. Remove from the heat, drain well, and transfer to a large, shallow ovenproof dish.

Preheat the oven to 450°F/230°C. Melt the butter in a small skillet over medium heat. Add the sliced mushrooms, stir to coat, and cook gently for 3 minutes. Remove from the heat and add to the cauliflower. Season with salt and pepper.

Combine the breadcrumbs, cheese, and herbs in a small mixing bowl, then sprinkle the crumbs over the vegetables.

Dice the butter for the topping and dot it over the crumbs. Place the dish in the oven and bake for 15 minutes, or until the crumbs are golden brown and crisp. Serve from the dish.

Caramelized Onion Tart

serves 4–6

7 tbsp unsalted butter

lb 5 oz/600 g onions, thinly sliced

2 eggs

scant ½ cup heavy cream

scant 1 cup grated Swiss cheese

8-inch/20-cm baked pie shell

generous 1 cup grated Parmesan cheese

salt and pepper

Melt the butter over medium heat in a heavy skillet. Stir in the onions and cook until they are well browned and caramelized. (This will take up to 30 minutes, depending on the width of the skillet.) Stir frequently to avoid burning. Remove the onions from the skillet and set aside.

Preheat the oven to 375°F/190°C.

Beat the eggs in a large mixing bowl, stir in the cream, and season with salt and pepper. Add the Swiss cheese and mix well. Mix in the cooked onions.

Pour the egg and onion mixture into the baked pie shell, sprinkle with Parmesan, and place on a baking sheet. Bake for 15–20 minutes, or until the filling has set and begun to brown.

Remove from the oven and let rest for at least 10 minutes. The tart can be served hot or let cool to room temperature.

Leek & Egg Mornay

serves 4

2 tbsp butter

4 leeks, trimmed and sliced

8 hard-boiled eggs, shelled and quartered

55 g/2 oz butter

55 g/2 oz plain flour

300 ml/10 fl oz milk

55 g/2 oz cheddar or Emmental cheese, grated

1 tsp whole grain mustard

cayenne pepper (optional)

salt and pepper

Melt the butter in a frying pan over medium heat, add the leeks and cook. Remove when soft and add to a baking dish. Arrange the egg quarters on top and season to taste.

Preheat the grill to high.

Meanwhile, melt the butter in a small pan over a medium heat. Gradually add the flour, stirring constantly until it has been absorbed. Still stirring, slowly add the milk, until blended. Bring the sauce to the boil, reduce the heat and simmer, stirring, until it thickens. Add the cheese, mustard and cayenne pepper (if using), stirring until well blended.

Pour the sauce over the eggs and leeks. Put the dish under the grill for 2–3 minutes. Serve when bubbling.

Cheese & Tomato Pizza

serves 4–6

9-inch/23-cm ready-made pizza base

fresh basil leaves, torn

for the tomato topping

2/3 cup crushed tomatoes

3 tbsp tomato paste

2 garlic cloves, crushed

pinch each of sugar, salt, and pepper

handful of cherry tomatoes

for the cheese topping

2/3 cup crushed tomatoes

3 tbsp tomato paste

4 oz/115 g jar roasted peppers, drained and thickly sliced

a few black olives

salt and pepper

4 oz/115 g firm mozzarella cheese, grated

2 oz/55 g Parmesan cheese, grated

Preheat the oven to 400°F/200°C. To make the tomato topping, mix the crushed tomatoes, tomato paste, garlic, sugar, and salt and pepper together in a bowl. Spread over the ready-made pizza base and scatter with the cherry tomatoes.

To make the cheese topping, mix the crushed tomatoes and tomato paste together in a bowl and spread over the pizza base. Top with the peppers and the olives. Season with salt and pepper and scatter the mozzarella and Parmesan cheeses over the top.

Bake in the oven for 8–10 minutes until hot and bubbling. Scatter with basil leaves and serve immediately.

Mozzarella Gnocchi

serves 2–4

butter, for greasing

1 lb/450 g package potato gnocchi

scant 1 cup heavy cream

8 oz/225 g firm mozzarella cheese, grated or chopped

salt and pepper

Preheat the broiler and grease a large baking dish.

Cook the gnocchi in a large pan of boiling salted water for about 3 minutes, or according to the package directions.

Drain and put into the prepared baking dish.

Season the cream with salt and pepper and drizzle over the gnocchi. Scatter over the cheese and cook under the broiler for a few minutes until the top is browned and bubbling. Serve immediately.

Vegetable Gratin

serves 4

1 lb/450 g mealy potatoes, peeled and diced

2 tbsp milk

¼ cup butter

2½ cups shredded green cabbage

1½ cups thinly sliced carrots

1 medium onion, chopped

½ cup grated cheddar cheese

salt and pepper

Cook the potatoes in salted water for 10 minutes, or until softened. Drain well and turn into a large mixing bowl. Mash until smooth. Beat with the milk, half the butter, and salt and pepper to taste.

Cook the cabbage and carrots separately in salted boiling water for 5 minutes. Drain well. Combine the cabbage with the potatoes. Melt the remaining butter in a small skillet and cook the onion over medium heat until softened but not browned.

Preheat the oven to 375°F/190°C.

Spread a layer of mashed potatoes in the bottom of a greased shallow ovenproof dish. Layer onions on top, then carrots. Repeat to use up all the ingredients, finishing with a layer of potato.

Sprinkle the grated cheese on top, place the dish in the oven, and bake for 45 minutes, or until the top is golden and crusty. Remove from the oven and serve immediately.

Leek & Spinach Pie

serves 6–8

8 oz/225 g puff pastry

2 tbsp unsalted butter

2 leeks, sliced finely

8 oz/225 g spinach, chopped

2 eggs

1¼ cups heavy cream

pinch of dried thyme

salt and pepper

Roll the pastry into a rectangle about 10 x 12 inches/ 25 x 30 cm. Let rest for 5 minutes, then press into a 8 x 10 inch/20 x 25 cm quiche pan. Do not trim the overhang. Cover the pastry with aluminum foil and chill in the refrigerator.

Preheat the oven to 350°F/180°C.

Melt the butter in a large skillet over medium heat. Add the leeks, stir, and cook gently for 5 minutes, or until soft. Add the spinach and cook for 3 minutes, or until soft. Let cool.

Beat the eggs in a bowl. Stir in the cream and season with thyme, salt, and pepper. Remove the pie shell from the refrigerator and uncover. Spread the cooked vegetables over the bottom. Pour in the egg mixture.

Place on a baking sheet and bake for 30 minutes, or until set. Remove the pie from the oven and let rest for 10 minutes before serving. Serve directly from the quiche pan.

Tofu Stir-Fry

serves 4

2 tbsp sunflower or olive oil

12 oz/350 g firm tofu, cubed

8 oz/225 g bok choy, coarsely chopped

1 garlic clove, chopped

4 tbsp sweet chili sauce

2 tbsp light soy sauce

Heat 1 tablespoon of oil in a wok, add the tofu in batches, and stir-fry for 2–3 minutes until golden. Remove and set aside.

Add the bok choy to the wok and stir-fry for a few seconds until tender and wilted. Remove and set aside.

Add the remaining oil to the wok, then add the garlic and stir-fry for 30 seconds.

Stir in the chili sauce and soy sauce and bring to a boil.

Return the tofu and bok choy to the wok and toss gently until coated in the sauce. Serve immediately.

Creamy Ricotta, Mint & Garlic Pasta

serves 4

10½ oz/300 g short fresh pasta shapes

heaping ½ cup ricotta cheese

1–2 roasted garlic cloves from a jar, finely chopped

⅔ cup heavy cream

1 tbsp chopped fresh mint, and 4 sprigs to garnish

salt and pepper

Cook the pasta in a large pan of boiling salted water for about 3 minutes, or according to the package directions until tender but still firm to the bite.

Beat the ricotta, garlic, cream, and chopped mint together in a bowl until smooth.

Drain the cooked pasta then tip back into the pan. Pour in the cheese mixture and toss together.

Season with pepper and serve immediately, garnished with the sprigs of mint.

Noodle Stir-Fry

serves 2

5 oz/140 g flat rice noodles

6 tbsp soy sauce

2 tbsp lemon juice

1 tsp granulated sugar

½ tsp cornstarch

1 tbsp vegetable oil

2 tsp grated fresh ginger

2 garlic cloves, chopped

4–5 scallions, trimmed and sliced

2 tbsp rice wine or dry sherry

7 oz/200 g canned water chestnuts, sliced

Put the noodles in a large bowl and cover with boiling water. Let stand for 4 minutes. Drain and rinse under cold running water.

Mix the soy sauce, lemon juice, sugar, and cornstarch together in small bowl.

Heat the oil in a wok, add the ginger and garlic, and stir-fry for 1 minute.

Add the scallions and stir-fry for 3 minutes.

Add the rice wine or dry sherry, followed by the soy sauce mixture and cook for 1 minute.

Stir in the water chestnuts and noodles and cook for an additional 1–2 minutes, or until heated through. Serve immediately.

Pasta with Olive Sauce

serves 2–4

12 oz/350 g fresh pasta shapes

6 tbsp olive oil

½ tsp freshly grated nutmeg

½ tsp black pepper

1 garlic clove, crushed

2 tbsp tapenade

½ cup black or green olives, pitted and sliced

1 tbsp chopped fresh parsley, to garnish (optional)

salt

Cook the pasta in a large pan of boiling salted water for about 4 minutes, or according to the package directions until tender but still firm to the bite.

Meanwhile, put ½ teaspoon of salt with the oil, nutmeg, pepper, garlic, tapenade, and olives in another saucepan and heat slowly but do not allow to boil. Cover and let stand for 3–4 minutes.

Drain the pasta and return to the pan. Add the olives in the flavored oil and heat gently for 1–2 minutes. Serve immediately, garnished with chopped parsley, if using.

Vegetable Chili

serves 4

1 eggplant, cut into 1-inch/2.5-cm slices

1 tbsp olive oil, plus extra for brushing

1 large red onion, finely chopped

2 red or yellow bell peppers, seeded and finely chopped

3–4 garlic cloves, finely chopped or crushed

1 lb 12 oz/800 g canned chopped tomatoes

1 tbsp mild chili powder

½ tsp ground cumin

½ tsp dried oregano

2 small zucchini, cut into fourths, lengthwise, and sliced

14 oz/400 g canned kidney beans, drained and rinsed

2 cups water

1 tbsp tomato paste

6 scallions, finely chopped

generous 1 cup grated cheddar cheese

salt and pepper

Brush the eggplant slices on one side with olive oil. Heat half the oil in a large, heavy-bottomed skillet over medium-high heat. Add the eggplant slices, oiled-side up, and cook for 5–6 minutes, or until browned on one side. Turn the slices over, cook on the other side until browned, and transfer to a plate. Cut into bite-size pieces.

Heat the remaining oil in a large pan over medium heat. Add the onion and bell peppers and cook, stirring occasionally, for 3–4 minutes, or until the onion is softened, but not browned.

Add the garlic and cook for an additional 2–3 minutes, or until the onion is beginning to color.

Add the tomatoes, chili powder, cumin, and oregano. Season to taste with salt and pepper. Bring just to a boil, reduce the heat, cover, and simmer gently for 15 minutes.

Add the zucchini, eggplant pieces, and kidney beans. Stir in the water and the tomato paste. Return to a boil, then cover and continue simmering for 45 minutes, or until the vegetables are tender. Taste and adjust the seasoning if necessary. Ladle into warmed serving bowls and top with scallions and cheese.

Spaghetti with Parsley & Parmesan

serves 4

1 lb/450 g dried spaghetti

¾ cup unsalted butter

4 tbsp chopped fresh
flat-leaf parsley

8 oz/225 g Parmesan
cheese, grated

salt

Cook the pasta in a large pan of boiling salted water for 10–12 minutes, or until tender but still firm to the bite. Drain and tip into a warmed serving dish.

Add the butter, parsley, and half the Parmesan cheese and toss well, using 2 forks, until the butter and cheese have melted. Sprinkle with the remaining Parmesan cheese and serve immediately.

Vegetarian Lasagne

serves 4

1½ oz/40 g dried porcini mushrooms

2 tbsp olive oil

1 onion, finely chopped

14 oz/400 g canned chopped tomatoes

¼ cup butter, plus extra for greasing

1 lb/450 g white mushrooms, thinly sliced

1 garlic clove, finely chopped

1 tbsp lemon juice

½ tsp Dijon mustard

jar of store-bought cheese sauce

6 sheets no-precook lasagne

½ cup freshly grated Parmesan cheese

salt and pepper

Preheat the oven to 400°F/200°C. Place the porcini mushrooms in a small bowl, cover with boiling water, and let soak for 30 minutes. Meanwhile, heat the oil in a small skillet. Add the chopped onion and cook, stirring occasionally, for 5 minutes, or until softened. Add the tomatoes and cook, stirring frequently, for 7–8 minutes. Season with salt and pepper and reserve.

Drain and slice the porcini mushrooms. Melt half the butter in a large, heavy-bottomed skillet. Add the porcini and white mushrooms and cook until they begin to release their juices. Add the garlic and lemon juice and season to taste with salt and pepper. Cook over low heat, stirring occasionally, until almost all the liquid has evaporated.

Lightly grease an ovenproof dish with butter. Stir the mustard into the cheese sauce, then spread a layer over the bottom of the dish. Place a layer of lasagne sheets on top, cover with the mushrooms, another layer of sauce, another layer of lasagne, the tomato mixture, and finally, another layer of sauce. Sprinkle with the Parmesan cheese and dot with the remaining butter. Bake in the preheated oven for 20 minutes. Let stand for 5 minutes before serving.

Cheese & Vegetable Tart

serves 4

12 oz/350 g prepared, unsweetened pie dough, thawed if frozen

10 oz/280 g mixed frozen vegetables

²/₃ cup heavy cream

4 oz/115 g cheddar cheese, grated

salt and pepper

Thinly roll out the dough on a lightly floured counter and use to line a 9-inch/23-cm tart pan. Prick the base and chill in the refrigerator for 30 minutes. Preheat the oven to 400°F/200°C.

Line the pastry shell with foil and half-fill with dried beans. Place the pan on a baking sheet and bake for 15–20 minutes, or until just firm. Remove the beans and foil, return the pastry shell to the oven, and bake for an additional 5–7 minutes until golden. Remove the pastry shell from the oven and let cool in the pan.

Meanwhile, cook the frozen vegetables in a pan of salted boiling water. Drain and let cool.

When ready to cook, preheat the oven again to 400°F/ 200°C. Mix the cooked vegetables and cream together and season with salt and pepper. Spoon the mixture evenly into the pastry shell and sprinkle with the cheese. Bake for 15 minutes, or until the cheese has melted and is turning golden. Serve hot or cold.

Pasta with Tomatoes & Spinach

serves 4

1 lb/450 g dried orecchiette or other pasta shapes

3 tbsp olive oil

8 oz/225 g fresh baby spinach leaves, tough stalks removed

1 lb/450 g cherry tomatoes, halved

Parmesan cheese, grated (optional)

salt and pepper

Cook the pasta in a large pan of boiling salted water for 10–12 minutes, or until tender but still firm to the bite.

Heat the oil in a pan, add the spinach and tomatoes, and cook, gently stirring occasionally, for 2–3 minutes, or until the spinach has wilted and the tomatoes are heated through but not disintegrating.

Drain the pasta and add it to the pan of vegetables. Toss gently, season with salt and pepper, sprinkle over some Parmesan cheese if using, and serve immediately.

Summer Stir-Fry

serves 4

4 oz/115 g green beans

4 oz/115 g snow peas

4 oz/115 g carrots

4 oz/115 g asparagus spears

½ red bell pepper

½ orange bell pepper

½ yellow bell pepper

2 celery stalks

3 scallions

2 tbsp peanut or corn oil

1 tsp finely chopped fresh ginger

2 garlic cloves, finely chopped

4 oz/115 g broccoli florets

salt

Chinese chives, to garnish

Slice the green beans, snow peas, carrots, asparagus, bell peppers, celery, and scallions and reserve. Heat half the oil in a preheated wok or heavy-bottomed skillet. Add the ginger and garlic and stir-fry for a few seconds, then add the green beans and stir-fry for 2 minutes.

Add the snow peas, stir-fry for 1 minute, then add the broccoli florets, carrots, and asparagus and stir-fry for 2 minutes.

Add the remaining oil, the bell peppers, celery, and scallions and stir-fry for a further 2–3 minutes, or until all the vegetables are crisp and tender. Season to taste with salt and serve immediately, garnished with Chinese chives.

4

Side
Dishes

Roasted Vegetables

serves 4

1 onion, cut into wedges

2–4 garlic cloves, left whole but peeled

1 eggplant, about 8 oz/ 225 g, trimmed and cut into cubes

2 zucchini, about 6 oz/ 175 g, trimmed and cut into chunks

10½ oz/300 g butternut squash, peeled, seeded, and cut into small wedges

2 assorted colored bell peppers, seeded and cut into chunks

2 tsp olive oil

1 tbsp shredded fresh basil

pepper

Preheat the oven to 400°F/200°C. Place the onion wedges, whole garlic cloves, and eggplant cubes in a large roasting pan.

Add the zucchini, squash, and peppers to the roasting pan then pour over the oil. Turn the vegetables until they are lightly coated in the oil.

Roast the vegetables for 35–40 minutes, or until softened but not mushy. Turn the vegetables over occasionally during cooking.

Remove the vegetables from the oven, season with pepper to taste, and stir. Scatter with shredded basil and serve divided among 4 warmed bowls while still warm.

Lemon & Garlic Spinach

serves 4

4 tbsp olive oil

2 garlic cloves, thinly sliced

1 lb/450 g fresh spinach,
torn or shredded

juice of ½ lemon

salt and pepper

Heat the olive oil in a large skillet over high heat. Add the garlic and spinach and cook, stirring constantly, until the spinach is softened. Take care not to let the spinach burn.

Remove from the heat, turn into a serving bowl, and sprinkle with lemon juice. Season with salt and pepper. Mix well and serve either hot or at room temperature.

Mixed Cabbage Coleslaw

serves 4

3 oz/85 g red cabbage

3 oz/85 g hard white cabbage

2 oz/55 g green cabbage

2 carrots, about 6 oz/175 g, peeled and grated

1 white onion, finely sliced

2 red apples, cored and chopped

4 tbsp orange juice

2 celery stalks, trimmed and finely sliced

2 oz/55 g canned corn kernels, drained

2 tbsp raisins

for the dressing

4 tbsp low-fat plain yogurt

1 tbsp chopped fresh parsley

pepper

Discard the outer leaves and hard central core from the cabbages and shred finely. Wash well in plenty of cold water and drain thoroughly.

Place the cabbages in a bowl and stir in the carrots and onion. Toss the apples in the orange juice and add to the cabbages together with any remaining orange juice, and the celery, corn, and raisins. Mix well.

For the dressing, mix the yogurt, parsley, and pepper to taste in a bowl then pour over the cabbage mixture. Stir and serve.

Chinese-Style Gingered Vegetables

serves 2

1 tbsp sunflower or peanut oil

1-inch/2.5-cm piece fresh ginger, peeled and grated

1 onion, thinly sliced

4 oz/115 g frozen green string beans, cut into small pieces

1 lb/450 g bag frozen mixed vegetables

²/₃ cup water

2 heaping tbsp dark brown sugar

2 tbsp cornstarch

4 tbsp vinegar

4 tbsp soy sauce

1 tsp ground ginger

Heat the oil in a wok or large skillet, add the grated ginger, and sauté for 1 minute. Remove from the wok or skillet and drain on paper towels.

Reduce the heat slightly and add the vegetables and water to the wok.

Cover with a lid or foil and cook for 5–6 minutes, or until the vegetables are tender.

Mix the sugar, cornstarch, vinegar, soy sauce, and ground ginger together in a bowl. Increase the heat to medium and add the mixture to the vegetables in the wok. Simmer for 1 minute, stirring, until thickened.

Return the ginger to the wok and stir to mix well. Heat through for 2 minutes and then serve immediately.

Crispy Roast Asparagus

serves 4

16 asparagus stalks

2 tbsp extra virgin olive oil

1 tsp coarse sea salt

1 tbsp grated Parmesan
cheese, to serve

Preheat the oven to 400°F/200°C.

Choose asparagus stalks of similar widths. Trim the base
of the stalks so that all the stems are approximately the
same length.

Arrange the asparagus in a single layer on a baking sheet.
Drizzle with olive oil and sprinkle with salt.

Place the baking sheet in the oven and bake for 10–15
minutes, turning once. Remove from the oven, transfer to
an attractive dish, and serve immediately, sprinkled with the
grated Parmesan.

Hot Roasted Bell Peppers

serves 6

6 red bell peppers, seeded and cut into thick strips

5 oz/140 g fresh green serrano or jalapeño chiles, seeded and sliced into thin strips

2 garlic cloves, crushed

4 tbsp extra virgin olive oil

Preheat the oven to 400°F/200°C. Put the peppers, chiles and garlic in a shallow casserole dish. Pour in the oil.

Cover and bake for 50–60 minutes, or until the peppers have softened. Remove the lid and reduce the temperature to 350°F/180°C. Return the casserole dish to the oven and bake for an additional 45 minutes, or until the peppers are very soft and beginning to char.

Serve immediately if serving hot. Alternatively, let cool, then transfer to a large screw-top jar and store in the refrigerator for up to 3 weeks, topped off with more olive oil to keep the peppers covered, if necessary.

Mexican Rice

serves 4

1 onion, chopped

14 oz/400 g plum tomatoes, peeled, seeded, and chopped

1 cup vegetable stock

1 cup long-grain rice

salt and pepper

Put the onion and tomatoes in a food processor and process to a smooth purée. Scrape the purée into a pan, pour in the stock, and bring to a boil over medium heat, stirring occasionally.

Add the rice and stir once, then reduce the heat, cover, and simmer for 20–25 minutes until all the liquid has been absorbed and the rice is tender. Season with salt and pepper to taste and serve immediately.

Spiced Lentils with Spinach

serves 4–6

2 tbsp olive oil

1 large onion, finely chopped

1 large garlic clove, crushed

½ tbsp ground cumin

½ tsp ground ginger

generous 1 cup Puy lentils

about 2½ cups vegetable stock

4 oz/115 g young spinach leaves

2 tbsp fresh mint leaves

1 tbsp fresh cilantro leaves

1 tbsp fresh flat-leaf parsley leaves

freshly squeezed lemon juice

salt and pepper

strips of lemon zest, to garnish

Heat the oil in a large skillet over medium heat. Add the onion and cook, stirring occasionally, for about 6 minutes. Stir in the garlic, cumin, and ginger and cook, stirring occasionally, until the onion starts to brown.

Stir in the lentils. Pour in enough stock to cover the lentils by 1 inch/2.5 cm and bring to a boil. Lower the heat and simmer for 20–30 minutes until the lentils are tender.

Meanwhile, rinse the spinach leaves in several changes of cold water and shake dry. Finely chop the mint, cilantro leaves, and parsley.

If there isn't any stock left in the skillet, add a little extra. Add the spinach and stir through until it just wilts. Stir in the mint, cilantro, and parsley. Adjust the seasoning, adding lemon juice and salt and pepper. Transfer to a serving bowl and serve, garnished with lemon zest.

Herby Potatoes & Onion

serves 4

2 lb/900 g waxy potatoes, cut into cubes

9 tbsp butter

1 red onion, cut into 8

2 garlic cloves, crushed

1 tsp lemon juice

2 tbsp chopped thyme

salt and pepper

Cook the cubed potatoes in a pan of boiling water for 10 minutes, then drain thoroughly.

Melt the butter in a large, heavy skillet and add the red onion wedges, garlic, and lemon juice. Cook, stirring constantly, for 2–3 minutes.

Add the potatoes to the pan and mix well to coat in the butter mixture.

Reduce the heat, cover, and cook for 25–30 minutes, or until the potatoes are golden brown and tender.

Sprinkle the chopped thyme over the top of the potatoes and season to taste with salt and pepper.

Transfer to a warm serving dish and serve immediately.

Colcannon

serves 4

8 oz/225 g green cabbage, shredded

5 tbsp milk

1½ cup diced mealy potatoes

1 large leek, chopped

pinch of grated nutmeg

1 tbsp butter, melted

salt and pepper

Cook the shredded cabbage in a pan of boiling salted water for 7–10 minutes. Drain thoroughly and set aside.

Meanwhile, in a separate pan, bring the milk to a boil and add the potatoes and leek. Reduce the heat and simmer for 15–20 minutes, or until they are cooked through.

Stir in the grated nutmeg and thoroughly mash the potatoes and leek together.

Add the drained cabbage to the mashed potato and leek mixture and mix well.

Spoon the mixture into a warmed serving dish, making a hollow in the center with the back of a spoon.

Pour the melted butter into the hollow and serve the colcannon immediately.

Potatoes Dauphinois

serves 4

1 tbsp butter

1 lb 8 oz/675 g waxy potatoes, sliced

2 garlic cloves, crushed

1 red onion, sliced

¾ cup grated Swiss cheese

1¼ cups heavy cream

salt and pepper

Lightly grease a 4-cup/1-liter shallow ovenproof dish with the butter.

Arrange a single layer of potato slices in the base of the prepared dish.

Top the potato slices with half the garlic, half the sliced red onion, and one third of the grated Swiss cheese. Season to taste with a little salt and pepper to taste.

Repeat the layers in exactly the same order, finishing with a layer of potatoes topped with grated cheese.

Pour the heavy cream over the top of the potatoes and cook them in a preheated oven, 350°F/180°C, for about 1½ hours, or until the potatoes are cooked through and the top is golden brown and crispy. Serve the potatoes at once, straight from the dish.

Garlic Mash

serves 4

2 lb/900 g mealy potatoes,
cut into chunks

8 garlic cloves, crushed

¾ cup milk

6 tbsp butter

pinch of freshly grated
nutmeg

salt and ground black
pepper

1 tbsp chopped fresh
flat-leaf parsley,
to garnish

Put the potatoes in a large pan. Add enough cold water to
cover and a pinch of salt. Bring to a boil and cook for
10 minutes. Add the garlic and cook for 10–15 minutes
more, until the potatoes are tender.

Drain the potatoes and garlic thoroughly, reserving
3 tablespoons of the cooking liquid.

Return the reserved liquid to the pan, add the milk, and
bring to simmering point. Add the butter and return the
potatoes and garlic to the pan. Mash thoroughly with a
potato masher.

Season to taste with nutmeg, salt and pepper and beat the
potato mixture with a wooden spoon until light and fluffy.
Garnish with flat-leaf parsley and serve immediately.

Pesto Potatoes

serves 4

2 lb/900 g small new potatoes

2¾ oz/75 g fresh basil

2 tbsp pine nuts

3 garlic cloves, crushed

½ cup olive oil

¾ cup freshly grated Parmesan cheese and romano cheese, mixed

salt and pepper

fresh basil sprigs, to garnish

Cook the potatoes in a pan of salted boiling water for 15 minutes or until tender. Drain well, transfer to a warm serving dish, and keep warm until required.

Meanwhile, put the basil, pine nuts, garlic, and a little salt and pepper to taste in a food processor. Blend for 30 seconds, adding the oil gradually, until the mixture is smooth.

Remove the mixture from the food processor and place in a mixing bowl. Stir in the grated Parmesan and romano cheeses and mix together.

Spoon the pesto sauce over the potatoes and mix well. Garnish with fresh basil sprigs and serve immediately.

Steamed Vegetable Parcels

serves 4

4 oz/115 g green beans

¾ cup snow peas

12 baby carrots

8 baby onions or shallots

12 baby turnips

8 radishes

4 thinly pared strips of lemon zest

4 tbsp unsalted butter or vegetarian margarine

4 tsp finely chopped fresh chervil

4 tbsp dry white wine

salt and ground black pepper

Cut out 4 double thickness rounds of waxed paper about 12 inches/30 cm in diameter.

Divide the green beans, snow peas, carrots, onions or shallots, turnips, radishes and lemon zest among the rounds, placing them on one half. Season to taste with salt and pepper and dot with the butter. Sprinkle with the chervil and drizzle with the wine. Fold over the double layer of paper, twisting the edges together to seal.

Bring a large pan of water to a boil and place a steamer on top. Put the parcels in the steamer, cover tightly, and steam for 8–10 minutes, then remove the parcels from the steamer and serve them immediately, to be unwrapped at table.

Peas with Baby Onions

serves 4

1 tbsp of unsalted butter

1 cup baby onions

2 lb/900 g fresh peas, shelled

½ cup water

2 tbsp all-purpose flour

⅔ cup heavy cream

1 tbsp chopped fresh parsley

1 tbsp lemon juice

salt and ground black pepper

Melt the butter in a large, heavy pan. Add the whole baby onions and cook, stirring occasionally, for 5 minutes. Add the peas and cook, stirring constantly, for a further 3 minutes, then add the measured water and bring to a boil. Lower the heat, partially cover, and simmer for 10 minutes.

Beat the flour into the cream. Remove the pan from the heat, stir in the cream mixture and parsley, and season to taste with salt and pepper.

Return the pan to the heat and cook, stirring gently but constantly, for about 3 minutes, until thickened.

Stir the lemon juice into the sauce and serve the peas immediately.

Chinese Vegetables

serves 4

2 tbsp peanut oil

4½ cups broccoli florets

1 tbsp chopped fresh ginger

2 onions, each cut into
8 pieces

3 celery stalks, sliced

6 oz/175 g young spinach

1½ cups snow peas

6 scallions, quartered

2 garlic cloves, crushed

2 tbsp light soy sauce

2 tsp superfine sugar

2 tbsp dry sherry

1 tbsp hoisin sauce

⅔ cup vegetable stock

Heat the peanut oil in a preheated wok until it is almost smoking.

Add the broccoli florets, chopped ginger, onions, and celery to the wok and cook for 1 minute.

Add the spinach, snow peas, scallions, and garlic and cook for 3–4 minutes.

Mix together the soy sauce, superfine sugar, sherry, hoisin sauce, and vegetable stock.

Pour the stock mixture into the wok, mixing thoroughly to coat all the vegetables.

Cover the wok and cook over medium heat for 2–3 minutes, or until the vegetables are cooked through, but are still crisp.

Transfer the Chinese vegetables to a warm serving dish and serve them immediately. If liked, use the vegetables to fill pancakes.

Chargrilled Vegetables

serves 6

2 sweet potatoes, sliced

3 zucchini, halved lengthwise

3 red bell peppers, seeded and cut into quarters

olive oil, for brushing

salt

for the salsa verde

2 fresh green chiles, halved and seeded

8 scallions, coarsely chopped

2 garlic cloves, coarsely chopped

1 tbsp capers

bunch of fresh parsley, coarsely chopped

grated rind and juice of 1 lime

4 tbsp lemon juice

6 tbsp olive oil

1 tbsp green Tabasco sauce

ground black pepper

Cook the sweet potato slices in boiling water for 5 minutes. Drain and let cool. Sprinkle the zucchini with salt and let stand for 30 minutes. Rinse and pat dry with paper towels.

Meanwhile, make the salsa verde. Put the chiles, scallions, and garlic in a food processor and process briefly. Add the capers and parsley and pulse until finely chopped. Transfer the mixture into a serving bowl.

Stir in the lime zest and juice, lemon juice, olive oil, and Tabasco. Season to taste with pepper, cover with plastic wrap, and chill in the refrigerator until required.

Brush the sweet potato slices, zucchini, and bell peppers with olive oil and spread out on a broiler rack or grill. Broil, turning once and brushing with more olive oil, for 8–10 minutes, until tender and lightly charred. Serve the vegetables immediately with the salsa verde.

Lemon Beans

serves 4

2 lb/900 g mixed green
beans, such as fava
beans, green beans, pole
beans

5 tbsp butter or margarine

4 tsp all-purpose flour

1¼ cups vegetable stock

5 tbsp dry white wine

6 tbsp light cream

3 tbsp chopped mixed
herbs

2 tbsp lemon juice

grated zest of 1 lemon

salt and pepper

Cook the beans in a pan of boiling salted water for
10 minutes, or until tender. Drain and place in a warmed
serving dish.

Meanwhile, melt the butter in a pan. Add the flour and cook,
stirring constantly, for 1 minute. Remove the pan from the
heat and gradually stir in the stock and wine. Return the
pan to the heat and bring to a boil, stirring.

Remove the pan from the heat once again and stir in the
light cream, mixed herbs, and lemon zest and juice. Season
with salt and pepper to taste. Pour the sauce over the
beans, mixing well to coat thoroughly. Serve immediately.

apples
    mixed cabbage coleslaw 129
    nutty beet salad 65
apricots
    hot garlic-stuffed mushrooms 45
    spicy stuffed bell peppers 54
arugula
    lettuce & arugula soup 22
    warm goat cheese salad 80
asparagus
    crispy roast asparagus 132
    filo-wrapped asparagus 24
    summer stir-fry 121

bamboo shoots: spring rolls 42
bean sprouts: spring rolls 42
beans
    mixed bean soup 21
    vegetable chili 110
beets
    borscht 15
    nutty beet salad 65
bell peppers
    bell pepper & basil stacks 27
    bell pepper & chile soup 18
    chargrilled vegetables 156
    cheese & tomato pizza 94
    hot roasted bell peppers 135
    Moroccan tomato & red pepper
        salad 83
    open potato omelet 59
    roasted vegetables 124
    spicy stuffed bell peppers 54
    summer stir-fry 121
    tomato ratatouille 56
    vegetable chili 110
    vegetable & corn chowder 10
    vegetable tartlets 36
broccoli
    chili broccoli pasta 86
    Chinese vegetables 154
    summer stir-fry 121
    vegetable & corn chowder 10

cabbage
    borscht 15
    colcannon 142
    mixed cabbage coleslaw 129
    vegetable gratin 98
carrots
    carrot & cumin soup 16
    lettuce & arugula soup 22
    mixed cabbage coleslaw 129
    potato, leek & feta patties 50
    steamed vegetable parcels 150
    summer stir-fry 121
    vegetable gratin 98
    zucchini, carrot & tomato
        frittata 53
cauliflower: mushroom & cauliflower
        cheese crumble 88
celery
    borscht 15
    carrot & cumin soup 16
    Chinese vegetables 154

mixed bean soup 21
mixed cabbage coleslaw 129
mushroom pâté 28
summer stir-fry 121
cheese
    baked chile cheese sandwiches 74
    broiled provolone with herbed
        couscous 77
    caramelized onion tart 91
    cheese baked zucchini 62
    cheese & tomato pizza 94
    cheese & vegetable tart 116
    creamy ricotta, mint & garlic
        pasta 104
    filo-wrapped asparagus 24
    green bean & walnut salad 60
    leek & egg mornay 92
    mozzarella gnocchi 97
    mushroom & cauliflower cheese
        crumble 88
    nachos with chiles & olives 78
    pesto potatoes 148
    potatoes dauphinois 144
    spaghetti with parsley &
        Parmesan 112
    stuffed eggplant slices 30
    vegetable & corn chowder 10
    vegetable gratin 98
    vegetarian lasagne 115
    see also feta cheese; goat cheese
chickpeas: falafel burgers 71
chiles
    baked chile cheese sandwiches 74
    bell pepper & chile soup 18
    chargrilled vegetables 156
    chili broccoli pasta 86
    hot roasted bell peppers 135
    mushroom pâté 28
    nachos with chiles & olives 78
    quesadillas 33
    spicy stuffed bell peppers 54
    vegetable chili 110
corn
    mixed cabbage coleslaw 129
    quesadillas 33
    vegetable & corn chowder 10

eggplants
    eggplant pâté 39
    roasted vegetables 124
    stuffed eggplant slices 30
    tomato ratatouille 56
    vegetable chili 110
eggs
    caramelized onion tart 91
    leek & egg mornay 92
    leek & spinach pie 100
    open potato omelette 59
    zucchini, carrot & tomato
        frittata 53

feta cheese
    hot garlic-stuffed mushrooms 45
    potato, leek & feta patties 50
    tomato & feta salad 66

goat cheese
    goat cheese tarts 68
    warm goat cheese salad 80
green beans
    Chinese-style gingered
        vegetables 130
    green bean & walnut salad 60
    lemon beans 159
    steamed vegetable parcels 150
    summer stir-fry 121

leeks
    colcannon 142
    leek & egg mornay 92
    leek & spinach pie 100
    lettuce & arugula soup 22
    potato, leek & feta patties 50
lentils: spiced lentils with
        spinach 138
lettuce & arugula soup 22

mushrooms
    creamed mushrooms 34
    hot garlic-stuffed mushrooms 45
    mushroom & cauliflower cheese
        crumble 88
    mushroom pâté 28
    spring rolls 42
    tomato ratatouille 56
    vegetarian lasagne 115

noodle stir-fry 106
nuts
    green bean & walnut salad 60
    nutty beet salad 65
    wilted spinach, yogurt & walnut
        salad 72

olives
    nachos with chiles & olives 78
    pasta with olive sauce 109
    tomato & feta salad 66

pasta
    chili broccoli pasta 86
    creamy ricotta, mint & garlic
        pasta 104
    pasta with olive sauce 109
    pasta with tomatoes &
        spinach 118
    spaghetti with parsley &
        Parmesan 112
    vegetarian lasagne 115
peas with baby onions 153
potatoes
    carrot & cumin soup 16
    colcannon 142
    garlic mash 147
    herby potatoes & onion 141
    mozzarella gnocchi 97
    open potato omelette 59
    pesto potatoes 148
    potatoes dauphinois 144
    vegetable & corn chowder 10
    vegetable gratin 98

rice
    lettuce & arugula soup 22
    Mexican rice 136
    spicy stuffed bell peppers 54

snow peas
    Chinese vegetables 154
    steamed vegetable parcels 150
    summer stir-fry 121
spinach
    Chinese vegetables 154
    leek & spinach pie 100
    lemon & garlic spinach 126
    pasta with tomatoes &
        spinach 118
    spiced lentils with spinach 138
    wilted spinach, yogurt & walnut
        salad 72
squash: roasted vegetables 124
sweet potatoes
    chargrilled vegetables 156
    potato, leek & feta patties 50

tofu stir-fry 103
tomatoes
    bell pepper & basil stacks 27
    bell pepper & chile soup 18
    borscht 15
    cheese baked zucchini 62
    cheese & tomato pizza 94
    chili broccoli pasta 86
    creamy tomato & basil soup 12
    Mexican rice 136
    mixed bean soup 21
    Moroccan tomato & red bell
        pepper salad 83
    open potato omelet 59
    pasta with tomatoes &
        spinach 118
    red onion, tomato & herb
        salad 48
    stuffed eggplant slices 30
    tomato bruschetta 40
    tomato & feta salad 66
    tomato ratatouille 56
    vegetable chili 110
    vegetable tartlets 36
    vegetarian lasagne 115
    zucchini, carrot & tomato
        frittata 53

water chestnuts: noodle stir-fry 106

zucchini
    chargrilled vegetables 156
    cheese baked zucchini 62
    mixed bean soup 21
    open potato omelette 59
    roasted vegetables 124
    spicy stuffed bell peppers 54
    tomato ratatouille 56
    vegetable chili 110
    zucchini, carrot & tomato
        frittata 53